Flooded

STUDY GUIDE

Other Helpful, Inspiring Resources from Nicki Koziarz

Flooded

THE 5 BEST DECISIONS TO MAKE WHEN LIFE IS HARD AND DOUBT IS RISING

Nicki Koziarz

BETHANYHOUSE

a division of Baker Publishing Group
Minneapolis, Minnesota

© 2021 by Nicki Koziarz

Published by Bethany House Publishers
11400 Hampshire Avenue South
Bloomington, Minnesota 55438
www.bethanyhouse.com

Bethany House Publishers is a division of
Baker Publishing Group, Grand Rapids, Michigan

Printed in the United States of America

ISBN 978-0-7642-3648-8 (trade paperback)

Cover design by Kara Klotz and Alison Fargason

The author is represented by the Brock, Inc. Agency.

21 22 23 24 25 26 27   7 6 5 4 3 2 1

Contents

Hey, there!

Welcome to the Flooded Study Guide. *I'm so glad you are here! We are about to have the best time studying the account of Noah at a deeper level.*

Just a quick little note with some helpful tips as you get started.

First, please note that this study guide is designed to go along with the book Flooded. *So if you don't have a copy yet, you might want to grab one before beginning.*

Second, there are videos that go along with this study. You don't have to watch the videos, but I highly recommend them. Plus, the Flooded Video Study *will give you a peek around the Fixer Upper Farm. This guide is designed for you to watch the videos before starting each week of the study. We even have a section for you to take notes during each session!*

Third, studies show that doing something like this with at least one other person is super helpful to staying committed. Not sure how to lead a study? No problem. I've got you covered at nicki koziarz.com/freebies, where you can download a free resource on how to lead a Bible study (with zero experience!) either in-person or online. Any question throughout the study that has an asterisk * next to it would make a great question for group discussion.

Fourth, and last, because this is starting to feel like a sermon with my three points (smiles): I'm really excited to walk through all this content with you. This is hard and holy work. Each day I ask you to write out one thing you are trusting God for. You can write the exact same thing every time, but write something. *We're building and strengthening your faith one day at a time.*

Ready? Let's do this!

Nicki

Humility, honor,
and hope
are some
of the greatest
by-products
of walking
with God.

Decision One:
To Walk with God

SESSION 1 VIDEO STUDY NOTES ....

Where Do We Start?

Read: Chapter 1 of *Flooded* and Genesis 5:28–31.

Write down one thing you are trusting God for today:

Verse-of-the-Week Daily Challenge: Read this out loud three times today to help memorize it.

> He said to them, "Because of your little faith. For truly, I say to you, if you have faith like a grain of mustard seed, you will say to this mountain, 'Move from here to there,' and it will move, and nothing will be impossible for you."
>
> Matthew 17:20

I love the first day of a new Bible study. The crispness of the unused pages. The hope for all I will learn. And the determination to stay focused for a few weeks on one subject of the Bible.

The reality is, as you are opening these pages today, there are things fighting for your attention. Your to-do list won't get shorter by the end of this. I know my laundry piles are staring at me.

Yet there's a longing to be still, just for a few minutes, isn't there? To grow. Change. And challenge your faith.

Can I just go ahead and give you permission to invest in yourself today and all the days to come during this study?

The only way to become spiritually healthy and stronger is by taking time to do the work your soul needs. I'm tired of us not believing holy work isn't worth it. It is.

You may not feel up to wrestling through some hard things, or maybe you do. Regardless of where we're all starting today, there is something I dare say we all need more of: *faith*.

I've come to understand that the opposite of faith is doubt. And defeating what doubt can do to a soul is our focus in this study.

What better person in the Bible to teach us about defeating doubt than a man named Noah?

He's my favorite teacher on this subject. He's taught me valuable lessons. And he's helped me understand there are decisions we can make that can defeat the destruction of doubt. These five decisions we can see through his journey are small and simple, but they have an impact that reaches into eternity.

Here's my question for you as we begin: *"How's your faith?"* It's not a question we ask ourselves very often. But our faith should always be increasing, not decreasing.

If we've found ourselves in a season of seeking faith, it's okay, we'll find faith. Or if we are feeling like we're in a season of settling, it's okay, we'll find faith that moves us. And if your faith feels fine, then let's try to go from fine to fulfilled.

In fact, let's start off today with a little self-evaluation of your faith. Here are a few questions I'd like for you to answer as we begin this process.

1. On a scale of 1 to 10 (10 being the best it's ever been), where would you say your faith is today? _____
2. Have you ever found yourself praying for someone and wondered if your prayers really mattered? Yes or No
3. Do you feel like you have a healthy perspective on what it means to obey God? Yes or No

4. What does it mean for you to obey God?

5. Who is someone whose faith inspires you?

Now that you've taken inventory of yourself, I always like to take inventory of how much I think I know about a passage of Scripture before I begin. This is helpful because at the end you'll be able to look back and see how much you've learned.

Most likely you have heard of Noah. You've heard of the ark, the animals, the flood, and the rainbow. In the space below, write down everything you know about Noah, and then below that, I want you to write down anything you want to know by the end of this study. There's no right or wrong answer to this.

What I know about Noah today:

* **What I want to know about Noah by the end of this study:**

I wish I could specifically see the things you want to know about Noah, because I know I had so many questions going into this. But I have to be honest. Even after studying Noah for almost a year, I still have questions. There are a lot of unknowns to the Scriptures we will study, and specifically to the account of Noah. But here's my promise: We will try to get as many questions answered as possible through this study. I will share with you the perspectives people have showed me on the meaning of the text and the hope that is tucked away in each part of Noah's story.

According to reference.com, the word *faith* appears 336 times in the King James Version of the Bible. In other versions, it is used more—the NIV uses it 458 times!

If you had to write a definition of faith, what would it be? Write it here:

Ever wonder why Bible studies look at either the Greek or Hebrew meaning of a word? Words don't always have the same nuance of meaning in every language. Plus, one word can have a range of meanings in one language that only partially overlap with how it might be translated in another language. When we study the Greek or Hebrew words of a text, in essence we are studying the original language used, which can help us apply it to our lives today.

In the Greek, the word for "faith" is *pistis*. Take a quick detour to your favorite internet browser and do a word search of what *pistis* means, and write it below:

No matter how we've defined our faith or how we are showing up today in this study as it relates to our faith, Noah is definitely a man who teaches us a thing or two about faith. Noah is a great example of faith being expressed as faithfulness: He was faithful to do what God told him to do *for 120 years*. Obedience can be tiring, and your faith can grow weary. But being faithful is like exercising your faith in the athletic training sense. It is a strain, but it's what it takes to make it stronger. Noah "trained" for 120 years!

So let's open our Bibles to the point we meet Noah and his family in Genesis 5, and see what God said.

It's crazy to me that we are only six chapters into Genesis, and the world seems to be falling apart already. Humans are messy. This is optional, but I encourage you to take time this week to read Genesis 1–5 to see how we went from creation to the flood in just five chapters.

Genesis 1	Genesis 2	Genesis 3	Genesis 4	Genesis 5
Creation	Man & woman	Sin enters	Cain kills Abel	Adam to Noah

From Adam to Noah there were ten generations. That's all it took. Ten generations for God to become incredibly grieved over humanity.

According to Genesis 5:28, who was Noah's father?

How old was he when Noah was born?

In verse 29, what did Noah's father say after naming Noah?

According to verse 31, how many years did Noah's father live?
    A. 500
    B. 777
    C. 595

There's much more to learn, but I want to keep things doable each day for you!

After reading chapter 1 of *Flooded*, use the space below to write down any quotes/verses that stood out to you, as well as your initial thoughts on the chapter.

* **Why do you think the human heart has not changed since Adam?**

* **What is one thing you learned in today's study?**

It's More Than a Mountain

Read: Chapter 2 of *Flooded* and Matthew 17:14–20.

Write down one thing you are trusting God for today:

Verse-of-the-Week Daily Challenge: Try to fill in the blanks without looking back.

> He said to them, "Because of your _____ _____. For truly, I say to you, if _____ have faith like a _____ of _____ seed, you will say to _____ _____, 'Move from _____ to _____,' and it will _____, and nothing _____ _____ _____ for you."
>
> Matthew 17:20

If you and I were sitting at a coffee shop right now together, I'd ask, "Are you a mountain or beach person?" You'd have to pick one. None of this, "Let me explain why I want both."

This question always tells me a lot about someone's personality.

Beach people tend to be more about the sun, swimming, and relaxing on the beach. Mountain people tend to be about the hikes, hills, and hot tubs. Regardless of what type of vacation person you are, today we are all mountain people.

But we're going to be discussing a different type of mountain—the spiritual ones.

One of the most important things we will do through this *Flooded Study Guide* is take the time to understand the verses I mention in the book a little deeper. We're going to devote one day of our study time each week to this process.

Today is the day.

Hopefully by now you have read chapter 1 of *Flooded*. If you haven't, you might want to head that way, read it, and then come back to this.

In chapter 1, we start to unpack the concept of mustard-seed faith. Remember, it's not the quantity of our faith; it's the quality.

Turn to Matthew 17:17. How does Jesus describe this generation?

    A. Strong

    B. Loving

    C. Kind

    D. Unbelieving

* **Why do you think Jesus called them this?**

They weren't just weak in faith, wanting to believe but not completely succeeding. They were *faithless*, hard of heart, *unwilling to hear*, unwilling to obey, unwilling to be taught. Kinda sobering to think about, huh?

In chapter 2 of *Flooded*, I share the difference between *disbelief* and *unbelief*. Write down your understanding of these two words:

Disbelief:

Unbelief:

What is in between disbelief and unbelief?

    A. Fear

    B. Frustrations

    C. Doubt

    D. Discouragement

Read Matthew 17:19. What question did the disciples ask?

On this drawing of mountain peaks, I want you to identify some of the mountains that have gotten in the way of your belief. The clearer you can name them, the better. (Ex: my marriage, my finances, my relationships, etc.)

* **What would it look like for you to have mustard-seed faith over those mountains?**

* **If you were going to explain Matthew 17:20 to someone, what would you say?**

Some people might read this passage and think the disciples' faith failed. I've been there too. Like the time I shared about in chapter 2 with my friend Kristi as we prayed over the man who was dying.

* **Write about a time when it felt like your faith was failing:**

This passage is a good reminder that while our faith may sometimes feel like it's failing, Jesus' never does. He steps in and does what He's going to do, regardless of our faith. The disciples tried to do what they could in faith, but then they brought the problem to Jesus. And He handled it.

Bring your mountain to Jesus today.

Ask Him what needs to happen for this mountain to move.

And then, let Him do what only He can do.

Write down any quotes, verses, or takeaways from chapter 2 of *Flooded*:

* Why do you struggle to believe God?

What is one thing you learned in today's study?

Favor

Read: Chapter 3 of *Flooded* and Genesis 6:1–9.

Write down one thing you are trusting God for today:

Verse-of-the-Week Daily Challenge: Try to fill in the blanks without looking back.

_____ to them, "_____ of your _____ _____. For _____, I say to ____, if ____ have _____ a ____ of _____ ____, you will say to ____ _____, 'Move from _____ to ____,' and it will _____, and nothing _____ _____ _____ for you."

Matthew ____:____

I have only one regret from the season I lost my mom. Just a few weeks after her diagnosis, her dad, my last living grandparent, passed away. Because my mom had a brain tumor, her cognitive level was around that of a five-year-old. It was hard to have conversations with her about things, but she was able to comprehend what happened and she was sad. I knew all of her side of the family would be gathering together to celebrate her dad's life, and for a moment I wondered if we could get my mom there. I even found a flight where we could leave early in the morning and be home before bedtime. I was going to suggest it to my dad, but he was overwhelmed with everything, so I put it aside.

Still, I knew my mom would want to be there and I think it would have been good closure for her many brothers and sisters to see her one last time. And I regret I didn't push for this one last hoorah for my mom.

I know now, it doesn't matter. But still, I wonder if we could have made it happen.

In today's reading of Genesis 6, you will see in verse 6, Moses, the author of this text, uses the word *regret* to describe how God felt about humanity. However, this isn't the same "regret" in the example of my mom. God never wonders about, questions, or second-guesses His decisions.

Let's unpack this. . . .

Read Genesis 1:31. How does God describe all that He had created?

    A. Awful

    B. Sinful

    C. Good

    D. Beautiful

Now, do a quick Google search of the Hebrew meaning for the word *regret*. (Hint: Biblehub.com is my favorite place to search for things like this.)

Write down everything you find:

Hopefully your research led you to see that the Hebrew word for *regret* is sometimes translated as the word "repent" and sometimes it is translated as "feel sorrow, be grieved." In this situation, God was grieved with humanity. And He knew something must be done to stop the evil that was running wild in this "good" world He had created.

According to Genesis 6:7, what did God say He needed to do?

Write out Genesis 6:8:

* **What do you think it means to see that "Noah found favor in the eyes of the LORD"?**

In Hebrew, this word is חֵן (*ḥēn*) **favor, grace**. As a verb it is used seventy-eight times in its various forms in the Old Testament. As a noun, it is translated as χάρις *charis* in the Greek (Septuagint) translation of the Old Testament, which is the word used throughout the New Testament for *grace*.

Only one other person is described in this same way in the Old Testament. Turn to Exodus 33:17. What is the name of this person?

In chapter 3 of *Flooded*, I shared my brother Mike's story and how unbelief eventually pushed him to the point of no return.

* **Who is someone in your life you've experienced something similar with?**

Write out any thoughts or takeaways you had on chapter 3 of *Flooded*:

* **What is one step you can take today to keep walking with God?**

What is one thing you learned in today's study?

To Walk with God

Read: Catch up on any reading you have left for the first three chapters.

Write down one thing you are trusting God for today:

Verse-of-the-Week Daily Challenge: *Write out this week's memory verse here. Bonus points if you head to social media and post a video of you quoting it! Tag me in the post and I'll give you a virtual high five!*

E ach week on day four of our study, we will spend some time unpacking the decision you read about in the chapters assigned. This day is designed to help you begin to understand "how" to live out each decision. I know these five decisions seem simple, and maybe you think you are already making them. But I encourage you to take time each week to dig deeper into these decisions so that they become part of your everyday decision-making routine.

Decision One: To walk with God

First, let's look back and remember where we initially see this decision made by Noah.

Write out Genesis 6:9:

* **What do you think it means that Noah is described as righteous and blameless?**

According to Genesis 5:24, who else "walked with God"?

 A. Methuselah
 B. Sons and daughters
 C. Jared
 D. Enoch

How was Enoch related to Noah?

✻ **When you think about your family legacy, how has it impacted your faith?**

Some of us have been in church since the womb, and others of us have just found our way to Jesus. Regardless of what type of upbringing you had, the choice to walk with God is ultimately ours to make. What can be so sneaky about this decision is that we can start to think that reading our devotions, going to church, or attending our weekly Bible study becomes the way we "walk with God." But I believe this is something deeper.

My friend Joy and I like to take long walks together. Often before school pickup we'll meet at our local park and walk one of the paths. During our walk, we talk—a lot. I don't think we have ever run out of things to talk about.

It's the same when we make this decision to walk with God. It still requires us showing up, doing the work, but it's not just a routine, and in fact, each time it might look different. Most of us think of a walk like this as a once-a-day rhythm, reading or studying our Bible first thing in the morning, but not investing a second thought into our souls the rest of the day. Walking with God means consciously thinking about Him being present throughout the day and *wanting* that.

What if we challenged our rhythm and found a consistent space in our lives where we walked with God throughout our day?

I think there are four main ways we can do this. Let's unpack each one:

#1. We walk with humility.

Humility is one of the by-products of walking with God.

God is not walking with us like an owner of a dog, pulling us on a leash to get us back in line each time we pull away. He walks with us like I walk with my friend Joy, as a friend. And while God is our friend, He is still our God. Which means we have an awe of wonder with Him that goes beyond a friendship. Humility allows us to remember this and not allow our thoughts, actions, and decisions to attempt to go higher than God. Humility allows us to stay in this posture before God.

Read Proverbs 22:4. What does this verse say the reward for humility and fear of the Lord is?

Do you think Noah experienced those things? Yes or No

#2. We walk with honor.

I think there are several ways we can walk with honor toward God all day long. The ones sticking out to me the most would be our time, our gifting, our bodies, and our finances.

Read Psalm 144:4. Why is it important to remember our days are passing when it comes to honoring God?

* **What would it have looked like for Noah to honor God in these areas?**

* **What are some other ways you can honor God?**

#3. We walk with hope.

I get really tired of people preaching the doom-and-gloom message about what it means to follow Jesus. For those of us who follow Jesus, we are carriers of the same hope Jesus brought to the earth.

Read 2 Corinthians 4:16–18. These verses are loaded with reminders of why we should walk with hope. List two of them:

1. _____

   _____

2. _____

   _____

How did Noah walk with hope?

#4. We walk with holy expectancy.

Walking by faith with God is anything but boring. When we walk with God, there should be a stirring of expectancy. We should be looking for ways to see Him move in our lives and in the lives of others.

* Read John 10:10. What does experiencing the abundant life that Jesus promised mean to you?

* What holy expectancy do you think Noah might have felt as he walked with God?

I hope as you unpacked these four ways to walk with God, it allows this decision to become a little clearer in your process.

What is your takeaway from this week's study?

* **What is something you learned this week about either yourself or Noah that surprised you?**

* **What's a question you are asking?**

* **What step will you take next week to walk with God?**

Stop listening
to negative thoughts
that sow doubt
and try to
destroy God's
goodness.

Decision Two:
To Listen
to God

Listening and Building

Read: Chapter 4 of *Flooded* and Genesis 6:10–17.

Write down one thing you are trusting God for today:

Verse-of-the-Week Daily Challenge: Write this verse on two or three sticky notes and put them somewhere you see them a lot.

> So faith comes from hearing, and hearing through the word of Christ.
>
> Romans 10:17

Not long ago I started a small study for some of our community's students in our home. I worked hard to prepare a lesson, thought creatively to keep things fun and interesting, and I prayed for the Holy Spirit to meet us in a special way. The study seemed to go well, and the students did a great job interacting with each other. Several parents reached out to thank me for leading and shared some encouraging words their students said. But a few days later I ran into one of the moms, and when I thanked her for allowing her student to attend, she quickly informed me he would not be back. It was boring for him, she said.

I simply smiled and said, "That's okay," and walked away.

Instead of brushing it off and leaning in to the positive comments, I played that one negative comment again and again as I replayed the entire night in my head looking for moments when he would have thought such a thing. But this isn't something new I do. I have consistently fought the negative-comment cycle in my mind.

Many physiological studies show that our brains are wired to look for negativity since birth. I have also heard psychologists say that one negative comment has about the same emotional impact as ten positive comments. In chapter 4 of *Flooded*, I share this quote:

What you listen to often becomes the house you live in.

I became so full of discouragement after this one comment. But I knew in order to press on in faith and finish teaching those students, I would have to silence that comment. I don't want to live in a house of doubt built by someone else. It is incredibly important as we build this house of faith in our lives that we stop listening to the doubt that is trying to destroy all of God's goodness.

Noah is a man who teaches us a lot of things, but I am impressed with his ability to silence the doubt and to listen to God.

* **What negative comment or memory do you find yourself replaying in your mind?**

* **Why do you think it's so much easier to replay the negative things rather than the positive?**

We will see a pattern with Noah. As I mentioned in the book, there are very few words of Noah in the Scriptures we can study. But there are actions. Lots of them. And actions stem from decisions. The decisions we make daily determine our steps. So let's study more of Noah's actions and see how it leads to . . .

Decision Two: To listen to God

Turn to Genesis 6:10 and circle the names of Noah's three sons mentioned there:

Abe   Peter   Saul   Samuel   Shem

Jesus   Ham   Levi   Japheth

What is the word Genesis 6:11–12 repeats three times to describe the earth? (Study note: I'm using the ESV translation.)

A. Violent
B. Corrupt
C. Angry
D. Unfaithful

What type of wood does God tell Noah to use in Genesis 6:14?

Before I took the time to study the process Noah went through, I had some major misconceptions about Noah. One being that he just knew how to do this. The Scriptures don't tell us Noah was a licensed ark-building contractor, but he had to be a really smart guy. One of those guys who just knows how to make things work.

Reminds me so much of my husband, Kris. He's made for the farm life because he just knows how to build things out of nothing. But Noah had to have used animals to haul materials, ropes to pull things together, and a rustic version of a crane. And most likely, he hired people to help him with this. Noah may have been the only human who was "walking with God," but he wasn't the only human who had ever built a boat.

In Genesis 6:14, what are the two instructions about the ark God gives?

Make _____ in the ark and _____ it inside and out with _____ .

Turn to Genesis 6:15 and fill in these boxes of what the text says the measurements were to be:

Length	Breadth	Height

How many decks was the ark supposed to have?

    A. 5
    B. 3
    C. 2
    D. 4

Where was the door supposed to be? (Read Genesis 6:16.)

Are you amazed at how specific God was with these instructions? I am. But what if Noah had decided he didn't really like these instructions and wanted to figure out a better way to do this? We're going to study more of these instructions this week, but jump down to Genesis 6:22.

What does it say the ultimate result was?

In chapter 4 we talk about what it means to listen when listening doesn't make much sense in the moment. Think of a time when you felt God leading you to do something that sounded pretty senseless.

* **Write about the experience below:**

* **What was the ultimate result of your obedience?**

Use the space below to write out any other thoughts or things you uncovered during your study time about these verses and/or chapter 4:

Do You Know What You Believe?

Read: Chapter 5 of *Flooded* and Romans 10:14–17.

Write down one thing you are trusting God for today:

Verse-of-the-Week Daily Challenge: Read this out loud three times today to help memorize it.

> So faith comes from hearing, and hearing through the word of Christ.
>
> Romans 10:17

It was a Sunday afternoon when the doorbell rang. Women from a local church were going door to door in our neighborhood to share about their church, which was a different faith from the one I grew up in. They asked some questions about my faith, and we entered into a conversation where I felt so uncomfortable. Mainly because my soul was full of questions like . . . *Nicki, do you even know what you believe?*

If I'm honest, in that moment I wasn't totally sure. I knew I was standing on the faith of my parents, my pastor, and my Bible study friends, but did I know what I believed?

One reason I truly believe Noah was able to walk with God and listen to God is because he was a man who had taken the time to define what he believed about God. The crazy thing is, Noah lived in a world where there were no books on theology, and there wasn't access to a YouTube sermon series on the entire Bible. The Bible had not even been written yet.

So how did Noah lean in, listen, and do all those instructions God gave him that we saw yesterday in our reading?

I don't know. And I wish I could tell you exactly how Noah knew what was right. But I know how to help you know what is right inside of your soul. If we're going to decide to listen to God, we're going to have to make some decisions about what we believe.

Remember on day two of our study guide, we're taking the time to unpack the verse we're hopefully memorizing for the week. Romans 10:17 is a powerful connection to decision number two: to listen to God.

Write out Romans 10:17 in your own words:

Go back to the previous page and circle the word that is repeated twice in this verse.

* **What does it mean to you that hearing comes through the word of Christ?**

One of my goals as your Bible study guide teacher is to help you think on your own. Some of you may want to dig further into this verse; others are ready to move on. For those of you who want to take this further, I encourage you to read through Romans 10 entirely. Use a website like biblehub.com and study the verses deeper.

I also highly recommend heading to YouTube and typing in the search box "Romans 10:17 teaching by David Guzik," and then listening to his short teaching on this verse.[1] Write down your thoughts/connections back to this verse as it relates to our process here with Noah.

The last thing I want us to spend some time on today has to do with something we talk about in chapter 5 of *Flooded*: spiritual disciplines. If you haven't read that part yet, pause here and do that now. In that chapter we are specifically looking at the spiritual discipline of silence. While there are varying opinions about how many spiritual disciplines we can see laid out in the Scriptures, there are three I'd like to offer you today to help build your faith, specifically with listening. Something important to remember about these spiritual disciplines is that these are all things Jesus modeled for us. And if Jesus did it, it's good for us too.

#1. Silence

Since we talk enough about this in chapter 5 and I offer you a little challenge there, I'll just leave this one here.

But if this is still something you want to study a little more, here are a few other verses for you to look up:

Habakkuk 2:20
Psalm 46:10
Luke 9:18

1. David Guzik, "Where Faith Comes From—Romans 10:17," https://www.youtube.com/watch?v=2mEauetLUoA.

#2. Meditating on God's Word

I'm not just trying to be an annoying teacher by having these verses-of-the-week each week. My goal is to help you meditate on God's Word so that when doubt enters your thoughts, you can quickly replace it with one of these verses combined with a decision. How do we meditate on the Word? We sit in silence and read. We listen for the Holy Spirit to nudge us toward something we need to hear. And we keep the Word close by.

Read Luke 4:1–13. What do you see in these verses that would have come from Jesus meditating on God's Word?

#3 Prayer

Maybe this one feels obvious. But my question is, how does it feel for you to pray right now? Often when we are in seasons of doubt, it's hard to pray. And that's okay to admit. But the more we do what we know is good for our souls, the more our faith will increase. Sometimes when I don't have the words to pray, I will pray prayers other people have written. There are tons of prayer books out there, so think about grabbing one if you are struggling with your prayers right now.

* **Read Luke 5:16. Why do you think Jesus withdrew from others to pray?**

There are many other biblical disciplines to practice. And all of them will help you be prepared for those moments when the doorbell rings and we need an answer for why we believe what we believe (1 Peter 3:15). But I really believe these three will help you a lot when it comes to working through decision two: to listen to God.

Write out any other thoughts you have on chapter 5 of *Flooded* and any closing reflections you have about today's study:

Kinds and Kinds and Stuff

Read: Chapter 6 of *Flooded* and Genesis 6:17–22.

Write down one thing you are trusting God for today:

Verse-of-the-Week Daily Challenge: Fill in the blanks without looking back.

So _____ comes from _____, and _____ through the _____ of

_____.

Romans 10:17

I think most of us have had one of two views on how many animals were actually on the ark prior to studying this. Either we think Noah had to save millions of animals or we think there must have been just a few to load up on the ark. The few perspectives most likely come from children's books where we as a culture have "cute-enized" the ark. Meaning, *Oh, look at all the cute little animals in the ark.* But unlike the animals on the Fixer Upper Farm, I am doubtful there was a lot of cuteness involved with this process.

More like lots of smells.

Now that we understand a little of what it would take to build the ark, let's spend some time looking at what went INTO the ark.

According to Genesis 6:18, who was to come into the ark?

    A. Noah and his sons

    B. Noah and his wife

    C. Noah, Noah's wife, and Noah's sons

    D. Noah, Noah's wife, and Noah's sons and their wives

* **What emotions might Noah have felt after learning who the only people would be in the ark with him?**

We are doing a lot of "studying" of these verses, but we can't forget the humanity side of this. These were real people, with real feelings, real emotions, and real doubts. While the Scriptures aren't telling us anything about what's happening behind the scenes through all this, we know there was a lot going on emotionally. You know there were frustrations and fears within Noah's family.

Lots of feelings and emotions also went into the ark.

But what about the animals?

Circle or highlight the word *kind* as you read this verse:

> Of the birds according to their kinds, and of the animals according to their kinds, of every creeping thing of the ground, according to its kind, two of every sort shall come in to you to keep them alive.
>
> Genesis 6:20

This word *kind* is incredibly important as we unpack this passage. **What is a "kind"?** The biblical concept of created "kind" probably most closely corresponds to the family level in modern-day taxonomy. A good rule of thumb is that if two things can breed together, then they are of the same created kind. It is a bit more complicated than that, but this is a good quick measure of a "kind."

Later we'll see that Noah was also instructed to bring seven pairs of certain animals, but let's start with what we see listed in in Genesis 6:20. It's almost impossible to know the exact number of animals that God tells Noah to keep alive. The good news is, he didn't have to worry at all about the animals in the water. They were good to go! The Ark Encounter scholars have suggested nearly seven thousand animals came on board.[1]

* **List your ideas of things Noah and his family needed to plan out for the animals.**

Currently, the Fixer Upper Farm has sixteen barnyard baby residents. They are a lot to keep up with! I can't even fathom the noise, the smells, and the feeding schedules for thousands of animals. Again, Noah had to be a very smart and creative man.

Just for fun, two questions.

* **#1. If you were going to be locked on an ark for over a year, what are some of the items you would *definitely have* to bring?**

* **#2. If you could have picked one animal to NOT go on the ark, which one would you have chosen?**

---

1. The Ark Encounter: https://arkencounter.com/animals/how-they-fit/.

Okay, so we have people, and we have the animals. Now, what else needed to go into the ark?

What does Genesis 6:21 tell Noah to do?

It is possible Noah could have grown some food on the ark during their long stay, but sunlight was limited.

But remember, Noah and his family had a long time to prepare for this journey. Prior to entering the ark, they likely dried and preserved fruits and vegetables. They also probably brought grains for food, as they are easier to store. Another possibility is that they had cows for milk and to make cheeses and other food.

While Scripture tells us that only people, animals, and food was to go into the ark, one other thing for sure went into that ark. Turn to the ESV translation of Hebrews 11:7 and fill in the blanks:

By _____ Noah, being _____ by God concerning events as yet _____, in reverent fear constructed an _____ for the saving of his _____. By this he condemned the world and _____ an _____ of the _____ that comes by _____.

Yes, faith. It went into the ark, and it would eventually emerge.

Same for you. Throughout this study process, faith is coming in, again and again. Eventually it will start to come out of you. I promise. Don't give up on this process. Just keep taking the next step and the next step. It's going to all come together. Watch and see.

* What is one thing you didn't know about Noah and the ark before this week's study?

Write down one takeaway or quote from chapter 6 of *Flooded*:

Walk and Listen

Read: Catch up on any reading you didn't finish this week!

Write down one thing you are trusting God for today:

Verse-of-the-Week Daily Challenge: Do something creative with the verse this week. Examples: make a graphic on your phone; draw it on a piece of paper; or for all my not-so-artistic friends, ask someone who IS artistic to draw it, paint it, or put it on a graphic for you. They will be honored you asked.

> So faith comes from hearing, and hearing through the word of Christ.
>
> Romans 10:17

It's day four of the study guide, which means it's time to start putting these decisions together! This is one of my favorite parts. Let's learn it and then let's do it. There are a few more things we need to unpack about how to listen to God. I think these tips will be very helpful as you continue to navigate your steps with God and listen to Him.

There are several places we see Noah living out his listening and obeying. Here are a few examples:

Genesis 6:22 says Noah did what? _____

Genesis 7:5 says Noah did what? _____

And from Genesis 7:16, Noah did what? _____

Hopefully you are seeing the same pattern I see: God commanded; Noah obeyed.

If it feels like you're in a season of doubt, it might be time to go back and do the last thing you are sure God showed you. This could be something like extending forgiveness to someone. Letting go of something. Staying committed to a situation. Trying something new. Or doing something that still feels impossible when you think about it.

When it comes to listening to God, there are a few things I want to make sure we are all on the same page about.

1. God will never tell you to do something that goes against His Word. In fact, it will align with His Word.

What does Proverbs 3:6 say about this?

What is an instance when you have seen someone say something was from God that they heard, but you knew it went against the Word?

2. God will never tell you do something that harms someone else or yourself. Remember, we have an enemy of our souls who often disguises himself as something good to deceive us.

According to 2 Corinthians 11:14, how does Satan disguise himself?

This isn't a fun question to ask, but can you recall when someone did something in the name of God that was harmful to themself or someone else? Yes or No

Okay. So keep those two things front and center at all times when it comes to the direction God gives us. But also, let's spend some time looking at all the possible ways God can speak to you. I don't like to put God into a box, because hello, He did speak through a donkey (Numbers 22:21–39). God can do anything, and I'm not about to limit the way He will speak to you personally.

But based on the Scriptures, there are a few ways we can listen for God to speak. Here are four I think we should unpack today.

#1. God speaks through the Bible.

According to 2 Timothy 3:16, what is all Scripture?

A. God-read
B. God-said
C. God-breathed
D. God-created

What does this mean to you as you *listen* to the Bible?

#2: God speaks through creation.

What does Romans 1:20 tell us about the way God speaks through creation?

How does creation help you listen to God?

#3: God speaks through others.

Read James 3:17. Who is someone in your life this verse describes?

#4: God speaks through the Holy Spirit.

Read Romans 8:26–27. What do these verses tell us about the Holy Spirit?

Okay, as we wrap up this week, there is one last thing I want you to do. When I'm trying to listen for God, I write down whatever comes to mind. So pause for a moment and pray. Ask the Lord to speak to you. And then write down whatever comes to mind. Besides your Target-run list. (Wink.)

* What God is saying to you?

Write down any takeaways from this week:

* What is one thing you studied this week that you want to remember?

When it's hard
to understand
God's ways,
trust His
character.

Decision Three:
To Rise Above the Doubt

Holy Confidence

Read: Chapter 7 of *Flooded* and Genesis 7:1–5.

Write down one thing you are trusting God for today:

Verse-of-the-Week Daily Challenge: Read this out loud three times today to help memorize it.

> For my thoughts are not your thoughts, neither are your ways my ways, declares the LORD.
>
> Isaiah 55:8

This week of our study is one of the most important—and it could be one of the hardest. Not because I'm about to make you do a theological deep-dive through Noah, but because we need to do a deep-dive through your soul.

I recently turned forty, and I really believe that for one of the first times in my life, I'm okay with who I am. Why did it take me forty years to get to this place?

I don't know.

There's a concept I want to teach you that has changed a lot inside me. I'm not here this week to pump you up with all the self-help tools or make you believe you can do anything. Because you know you can't. We all have limits, but sometimes we also need to defy those limits.

There is a stretching God is doing in each of us today. It's moving us from complacent to courageous.

Let's look again to Noah, his process, and what the account of his life can teach us.

Circle or highlight key words that stand out to you in this verse:

Then the LORD said to Noah, "Go into the ark, you and all your household, for I have seen that you are righteous before me in this generation."

Genesis 7:1

Head to your favorite Bible translation website (Biblehub.com is my favorite) and read a few different versions of Genesis 7:1.

Write down any key words that are translated differently and how they connect with you.

A few things in this verse stand out to me. First, the reality that God told Noah it was time to go into the ark. I think we often rush ahead of God, especially when we are wrestling with doubt. In the book I shared this quote: "The timing of God is never hurried by the impatience of man."

* **When it comes to doubt, what are some examples you can think of where doubt could convince us to rush ahead of God?**

Another thing that stands out to me about Genesis 7:1 is that this is the second time we see God affirm over Noah that he was the only one found righteous. But this comes after about 120 years of obedience. Noah wasn't just faithful with a onetime obedience. It was a day-by-day, year-by-year decision.

In chapter 7 of *Flooded*, we cover the naysayers around us. But today, I want us to talk about our inner naysayer and how to silence it. Let's go back to the word *righteous* and see why this is the second time God is using this to describe Noah, and possibly what we need to understand more about this word.

Merriam-Webster defines *righteous* as "acting in accord with divine or moral law: free from guilt or sin."[1]

When we think about our lives and what it means to be righteous, it really comes down to this . . . obedience. The Hebrew word for *righteous* is *ṣaddîq*, which means both "just" and "righteous." The same thing happens in Greek, and in Latin, and some other languages. Being *just* relates to the social dimension—our relationship with others. Being *righteous* is more oriented toward the inward character.

Read Titus 3:6–7. Where does our righteousness come from?

    A. The Bible

    B. Jesus Christ

    C. Prayer

    D. Going to church

Read 2 Timothy 2:22. What does it say we should do to have righteousness in our life?

---

1. Definition found at https://www.merriam-webster.com/dictionary/righteous.

* **According to that verse, what else should we pursue?**

The thing that has helped me the most in learning to rise above my own doubt in my life? A holy confidence. Righteousness should help us have a holy confidence. Not because of anything we have done, but because of all that has been done for us through Jesus. We won't always get it right. But part of our growth process is recognizing this. We're not after perfection. You know that.

* **In what areas do you struggle to have a holy confidence?**

* **What would it look like for you to have holy confidence in those things?**

The reality is, we are our own worst enemy sometimes. We're the biggest naysayer in our lives. But it's so much easier to call out other people who are naysayers and not ourselves. As we wrap up today and head into the rest of this week, spend time today just sitting with God. Even if it's just two minutes. Ask Him to reveal the way you've been your own naysayer, and ask Him to show you how to build a holy confidence and righteousness in your life.

Write down anything that comes to mind during this time:

Write down any other takeaways you had from today's study:

When God Doesn't Do What You Want

Read: Chapter 8 of *Flooded* and Isaiah 55:1–11.

Write down one thing you are trusting God for today:

Verse-of-the-Week Daily Challenge: Try to quote it from memory.

> For my thoughts are not your thoughts, neither are your ways my ways, declares the LORD.
>
> Isaiah 55:8

What is your reaction when God does something you don't like?

It's the question we really need to wrestle through if we're going to get a hold on what doubt can do to someone's soul. Because most of the time, doubt stems from something we feel incredibly disappointed about. I imagine at some point Noah felt some disappointment about his assignment to build and then enter the ark.

I'm sure it was hard to process all the things he was leaving behind and the unknown new world he would be stepping into.

He also had a family to lead. They were counting on him and believed in him.

Still, I'm sure there were many conversations about whether this was the best way for God to do things.

While it's fine to wonder about and consider the ways of God, there does have to come a point where we are willing to rest in it all. Which is why our verse this week is so important to memorize and keep close to our souls when doubt starts to enter in. When it's hard for us to understand God's ways, we can still trust His character. He has never failed us, and He never will, despite any story doubt could tell us.

One way to unpack a verse deeper is by studying verses that are considered cross-references. The following two verses are cross-references to Isaiah 55:8 and might help your understanding.

Turn to Psalm 33:11 and fill in the blanks:

The _____ of the LORD _____ forever, the _____ of his _____ to all _____.

Psalm 33:11

How many generations will God's plans stand through?

A. One thousand

B. Ten thousand

C. All

D. Only the ones He picks

* **According to Isaiah 14:24, what does God promise about His plans?**

* **What does it mean to you personally when Isaiah 55:8 says God's thoughts and ways are higher than ours?**

There's something comforting and unsettling about this for me. I'm not a huge planner, but I do like to know what is happening. Communication is one of my top strengths, so when I start to feel like there's a breakdown in communication in my relationships, things feel messy to me. This is why each decision we are unpacking in this study guide, as well as the book, build on one another. When we walk with God, we listen to God, and when we listen to God, we remember that His ways and His thoughts are higher than ours. Which leads us to . . .

Decision Three: to rise above the doubt

In order for me to write about my own story of doubt, I have to remember the story of faith God is writing. *On the chart below, list places in your life where you have struggled to believe God's ways and thoughts as higher than yours. I encourage you to identify Scriptures to connect with God's thoughts and God's ways.

My Thoughts *Ex: I'm not enough*	God's Thoughts *We are more than conquerors (Romans 8:37*

My Ways	God's Ways
Ex: Controlling a situation	*He is sovereign (Ephesians 1:11)*

Write down any other thoughts or takeaways you had from chapter 8 of *Flooded*:

Closed Doors

Read: Chapter 9 of *Flooded* and Genesis 7:6–16.

Write down one thing you are trusting God for today:

Verse-of-the-Week Daily Challenge: Call a friend and explain what you have learned about Isaiah 55:8.

> For my thoughts are not your thoughts, neither are your ways my ways, declares the LORD.
>
> Isaiah 55:8

In chapter 9 of *Flooded*, we cover the significance of the number forty in the Bible. I even asked you to choose a forty-day challenge for yourself, so hopefully you are ready to start that! So we're going to skip down a few verses because there's a lot I need to share with you. These eleven verses (Genesis 7:6–16) have a lot to unpack. Stick with me. It's a study day!

Answer the following questions based on Genesis 7:6–10.

How old was Noah when God commanded him to go into the ark?

A. 600

B. 500

C. 400

D. 60

We will see that after the flood, people didn't live as long as they did pre-flood. I'm amazed at Noah's age, his endurance, and how much wisdom his life had taught him until this point. In our culture today, growing older isn't always seen as something to aspire toward. But a lot of good things come with growing older.

* **What benefits did Noah's age provide for an assignment like this?**

* **What benefits do you see for your own life as you grow older as it relates to your faith and trust in God?**

Read Genesis 7:8–10 and answer the following three questions.

What are the next four things to enter the ark in Genesis 7:8?

1. _____

2. _____

3. _____

4. _____

Do you know the difference between clean and unclean animals? Yes or No

How do these verses describe the animals entering the ark? Circle all that apply.

    A. One by one

    B. Male and female

    C. Male and male

    D. Female and female

    E. Two by two

In chapter 9 of *Flooded*, we look at Genesis 7:16b briefly. What did God do to the door?

* **What was significant to you about God being the one to shut the ark's door?**

    This is honestly one of my favorite parts of Noah's account. To know that God would be the one to close the door is both grace and mercy in the midst of a hopeless, hard situation. I think about the times in my life when God has clearly closed a door and I didn't have a clear understanding why. If I'm honest, sometimes when I think about those closed doors, it still hurts a little. But when I see in these verses the ways Noah decided to rise above his own self-doubt and listen to God, I'm encouraged and challenged.

    We may trust God to close the door, but do we trust Him enough to not try to open that door ourselves?

    After everyone in Noah's family was on the ark, I wonder if there were any knocks on the door? Did other people change their mind about the message Noah had preached the previous years and now they wanted to get in the ark?

This could have been the hardest part—keeping the door closed. Because they knew what God had commanded; they knew God had closed the door. But now it was up to them to keep it closed.

* **What is an example of a door in your life that is closed, but you keep thinking about opening it back up?**

* **What would happen if you opened that door?**

* **What could have happened to Noah, his family, and all the animals if he had opened the door?**

Sometimes closed doors feel like death. But as we will discover with Noah, there's more to closed doors than we can see right now. When I was studying this, I kept thinking of Psalm 23:4. End today's study by reading it and thanking God for the doors He has closed and affirming your trust in His ways, His timing, and His plans.

Write down any takeaways from today's study:

How Will You Know?

Read: Catch up on any reading you missed for the week!

Write down one thing you are trusting God for today:

Verse-of-the-Week Daily Challenge: Write out Isaiah 55:8 below.

hapter 9 is filled with great insights on finding your forty-day challenge and reminding the enemy that there is more of God's goodness where it came from. But there's one last concept I want to help you understand as it relates to our struggles to rise above doubt.

When we don't know who we are here for and what we are doing, doubt becomes a cycle we find ourselves in again and again. We need direction and hope.

Sometimes we find ourselves in situations where it feels impossible to have wisdom, direction, and discernment about what to do next.

While we don't have any other instructions to study from Noah right now, I want us to turn to decision number three: to rise above doubt.

Some of you are finishing this week and are unsure what your assignment of faith is right now. I want you to know, it's okay. There are seasons when it will be clear what you need to do and others when it feels a little foggy. Be careful, though, in those foggy seasons because doubt can start to write a story of complacency. Meaning, we settle and just don't care anymore.

Set a timer for three minutes and think through this last year of your life. Write down any circumstance that comes to mind where doubt tried to convince you to give up. What were the lies doubt shouted?

One way I believe we rise above doubt is by affirming God in our lives. Write down at least three affirmations about who God says you are. *Ex: God says I am loved by Him.*

1. _____
2. _____
3. _____

* **Who else in the Bible inspires you to rise above doubt?**

Doubt is something we have to choose to rise above again and again. It's not a one-and-done situation. But you are doing the hard work here, and remember, hard work is holy work. Keep going.

A few questions as we wrap up this third week of our study guide:

* What did you learn this week that surprised you?

On a scale of 1 to 10, with 10 being the worst it's ever been, how much doubt are you dealing with right now? _____

What is one takeaway you have from this week of study?

God has
the command
and the plan.
Our obedience
is what's at stake.

Decision Four:
To Remember Who Is in Charge

....

....

....

....

....

....

....

....

....

Water and Remember

Read: Chapter 10 of *Flooded* and Genesis 7:17–24; 8:1.

Write down one thing you are trusting God for today:

Verse-of-the-Week Daily Challenge: Write this verse three times in your journal or elsewhere.

> The LORD sits enthroned over the flood; the LORD sits enthroned as king forever.
>
> Psalm 29:10

This week's study is going to be valuable if you hate being bossed around. Hand raised. I mean, I'm all about clear expectations, clear roles, and clear assignments, but I do not like it when someone tells me what to do. Can you relate?

Decision Four: To remember Who is in charge

As we start to work through this decision, we might have a little bit of an unhealthy perspective about God and the way He leads us. Hopefully after reading chapter 10, specifically the coach example, we understand more clearly how God *leads* us. Not bosses us around. Although, sometimes it can feel like He's being bossy because often He shows us the same thing again and again.

A question for you . . .

* **Have you played any team sports during your life?** Yes or No

* **If yes, who are a few coaches you remember? If no, who is someone you know who is a coach?**

* **What stands out to you the most about them?**

As I continue to read Noah's account in Genesis 7, I see even more reasons why Noah needed to trust God's plan and His commands. Sure, Noah was busy taking care of the animals and helping his family get settled, but there was so much happening in and around him after the door closed. One general misconception about the flood is that the water came from a storm. This was part of it, but let's make sure we see one other place the waters came from.

Genesis 7:11 says the waters burst from _____.

I don't know what it's like when water bursts from the earth, but I do know about living near a hundred-year flood plain that floods at least a few times a year. The water rises so quickly. Usually just hours after a heavy rainstorm, the road leading to the Fixer Upper Farm totally floods. The earth is big, but for Noah, I imagine it would only have been a matter of hours before everything was wiped out.

What does Genesis 7:17 say happened to the ark during those forty days?

A. Sank to the bottom

B. Rose above the earth

C. Floated up on the mountains

After reading Genesis 7:17–24, write down all the facts mentioned. Try to find at least five.

1. _____

2. _____

3. _____

4. _____

5. _____

This is the part in our study where it all becomes incredibly sobering to me, thinking about the men, women, children, and animals who were not on the ark. The fear they experienced, while it may have only been for a few moments . . . still, it has me wondering again, *"God, was there not a better way?"* This connects back to last week, when we talked about God doing some things we just don't like.

But we can question His ways without questioning who He is.

Remember, Noah's account can either be seen as God's meanness or God's mercy. It's hard. I know. I feel very human right now typing these words, because it's sad to think about all the destruction.

But perhaps this part of Noah's account *should* feel weighty. I'm not sure we should study something like this and still feel good about ourselves. There are times when remembering that God is in charge feels incredibly hard and humbling.

But then, after Genesis 7, comes one of the best verses in this passage.

Write out Genesis 8:1:

* After reading chapter 10 of *Flooded*, specifically the part about how God remembers, how does this connect with you? Did you ever think about this concept before?

* What are some examples in your life of God "remembering" or acting on your behalf?

While there is much in this account to makes us wonder about God's ways, it should also be comforting. No matter what doubt tries to convince us about God, He has not forgotten us. It comes down to timing and trust as to when He will work on our behalf. Don't give up on this important decision to remember Who is in charge. He's got the plan and the command. Our obedience is what's at stake.

What is one thing you learned today?

Glory in Storms

Read: Chapter 11 of *Flooded* and Psalm 29.

Write down one thing you are trusting God for today:

Verse-of-the-Week Daily Challenge: Fill in the missing blanks to help memorize the verse.

> The LORD sits _____ over _____ _____; the LORD sits _____ as king forever.
>
> Psalm 29:10

I don't know about you, but I'm really loving these study days when we spend time unpacking our verse of the week. It's one thing to know a verse is important. It's another thing to really take the time to understand it. Some Bible scholars believe that David, the author of Psalm 29, might have penned the psalm during a storm and that it is about a flood the storm caused. However, one thing that suggests he is talking about *the* flood of Noah's time is the use of the definite article *the*, as though it were a specific flood that was known to many people. He also doesn't refer to *floods* (with an *s*). The word is singular, meaning a particular flood.

Doubts about God often come up during the storms of our lives.

It's easy to trust God when life is simple and smooth. But when things feel complicated and challenging, it's not only hard to trust that God is in charge, it's hard to believe anything good will come from it all.

Yesterday, I was very honest with you about how I feel reading about the destruction of human and animals that took place during the flood. In the book, I'm very honest about how I felt losing my mom and my brother and our horse in such a short span. Often a person can muster the emotional resources to deal with one crisis, especially if they have some time to prepare for it, such as losing a loved one to cancer, because you see it coming.

But it's often a second crisis in a short time that is so devastating, especially if the crisis is sudden or violent, or, worse, self-inflicted. Even losing a pet after losing a friend or family member can hit us really hard.

It is like a co-carcinogen being added to a carcinogen. A carcinogen is a cancer-causing agent, and a co-carcinogen is something that makes the effect of a carcinogen much more powerful. For me, it was the second and third blows that made the three together so much worse.

It's those "Why God, why me, why this . . ." questions that seem to set us on our way toward unbelief.

But let's see how Psalm 29 can help us trust God when things feel out of control.

In Psalm 29, note how many times the word *glory* appears in the eleven verses:

* **What else stood out to you from Psalm 29?**

Something interesting about the Hebrew meaning of the word *kavod*, which translates into *glory*: The root meaning is "heaviness," which can also refer to a physical weight or something serious or weighty spiritually. Most of the time when we picture the word *glory*, we think of bright and joyful, right?

Read Psalm 3:3. What does it mean to you personally to say God is your glory in the midst of a battle?

So, there's the *kavod* glory, but another type of glory that isn't directly found in the Scriptures is called *shekinah*. It is related to the word for tabernacle, which is where God's glory (*kavod*) was manifested in passages such as Exodus 24:15 and Exodus 44:34–35. This would be the picture of glory that is bright and awe-inspiring.

As I said, some Bible scholars believe David was connecting Psalm 29:10 back to the flood in Genesis. Some don't. Regardless, the passage does refer to God's victory over *chaotic forces*, of which turbulent waters is a great example.

The flood is an extreme display of God's glory. But it feels heavy and weighty, doesn't it?

Maybe one reason doubt feels so heavy in our soul is because pushing through it could bring about some of God's greatest glory in our lives. It's something to consider when we don't think it's worth it to press on and keep fighting doubt. There's more at stake than we may realize.

Another key word in some translations of Psalm 29:10 is *enthroned*, which appears twice. It means to sit, remain, or dwell.

What do you think it means in Psalm 29:10 that God is enthroned over the flood?

* What does it mean to you to believe that God is enthroned over your life?

What would it look for you personally to display God's glory in the midst of your doubt?

As we close out our study of Psalm 29:10, it might be hard to think about God getting glory through circumstances where doubt has tried to destroy our belief. But the comforting place is knowing and believing that God is in charge of everything, even the flood. He sits in a position that allows Him to see things from a perspective we don't have. And while the humanity side of us often wants to resist this process, remember, God sits enthroned over the flood, regardless of what we do, say, or . . . believe.

What are your takeaways from today's study?

What is something new you learned so far this week?

When the Storm Stops

Read: Chapter 12 of *Flooded* and Genesis 8:2–17.

Write down one thing you are trusting God for today:

Verse-of-the-Week Daily Challenge: Write each word of Psalm 29:10 on a separate index card or piece of paper, and then put the words in order a few times.

> The LORD sits enthroned over the flood; the LORD sits enthroned as king forever.
>
> Psalm 29:10

One of my favorite things about summers on the Fixer Upper Farm are the pop-up rainstorms that come through so unexpectedly. I especially love them when I'm down at our little white barn, because hearing rain hit the tin roof is pure delight. And when the tin stops clicking from raindrops, I know the storm has passed.

I'm not sure whether Noah and his family could hear the rain on the ark or not. But there was something they for sure experienced as a sign to know the storm was over: the wind. We look at this throughout chapter 11 in *Flooded*. But let's recap things a little, and then we have a lot of studying to do today!

Turn to Genesis 8:2. What two things happened to stop the water?

A. The sun came out, and the rain stopped.

B. The rain stopped, and God commanded the waters to dry up.

C. The springs and floodgates closed, and the rain stopped.

How does Genesis 8:3 describe the water receding?

A. Slowly

B. Continually/steadily

C. Incredibly fast

I'm not a scientist, but from what I've seen from the flooding we've had here on our farm, things change after a flood. The ground is shaped and formed. Things are moved very quickly. Think about what the earth would have looked like after water has covered it for somewhere around 150 days. Circle what would have been impacted by the flood:

Trees	Rivers	Lakes	Oceans	The atmosphere
Rocks	Bugs	Flowers	Grass	Mountains
Seas	Land	Dirt	Creatures	

Hopefully you circled everything. Even though sea creatures would not have been greatly affected by rising water, receding water did cause damage. Which is why many fossils of sea creatures have been discovered in rocks and canyons all these years later.

Turn to Genesis 8:4. Which mountains did the ark come to rest on?

Put these in order, 1 to 6, based on Genesis 8:6–12:

___ Noah sends out the dove.

___ Noah opens the window.

___ Noah sends out the raven.

___ Noah waits seven days and sends the dove out again.

___ Noah sends out the dove again, and she does not return.

___ Noah waits another seven days.

* **What do you think would have been the hardest part about waiting for a sign that the land was dry?**

In Genesis 8:13, Noah sees ground for the first time in almost a year. How do you think that might have felt for Noah?

At this point in the account, I'm sure Noah and his family experienced all kinds of emotions and feelings. Their bodies alone were probably in shock a bit. Have you ever gone on a cruise or a long boat ride? When you get off, you feel something called disembarkment syndrome. It's this feeling like you are still in motion, and when you lie down to sleep or even try to walk, it still feels like you're being moved by waves. It's such a crazy feeling!

I also wonder, even though Noah was told by God that no one else would survive the flood, whether Noah or his family wondered if somehow someone had made it through. Was there a little hope or expectancy that they would find other people alive? I don't know. I would have wondered, for sure.

Regardless, finally in Genesis 8:16, God gives them the command to exit the ark. And then began the massive assignment of getting everyone unloaded from the ark. I'm sure those animals were feeling a little anxious. Still, there had to be order and a system.

Some people who have studied this in depth wonder if Noah could have cut more openings in the ark besides the door to help get every animal unloaded quicker. It's possible, but again, we don't know for sure.

Turn to Genesis 8:17. What is the last command God gives for the animals?

Turn to Genesis 1:28. What did God say to Adam and Eve?

Making the decision to remember that God is in charge will help us get to the point where Noah found himself: the end of the storm. Life may feel like a prolonged trial or that everything is unpredictable, but the sun will shine again. We will step out onto dry land. And God will multiply what we walked through when we let Him use it for His glory. But let's check in tomorrow and see how to practically start making this decision again and again.

* **Are you in a storm that feels like it "won't end"?**

Or, can you think of a storm you went through that felt that way?

Write down any takeaways from today's lesson:

When You Still Want to Be in Charge

Read: Catch up on any reading you missed during the week.

Write down one thing you are trusting God for today:

Verse-of-the-Week Daily Challenge: Write out Psalm 29:10 from memory.

I love studying personalities. The Enneagram test is one of my favorite things right now to help understand people around me. If you aren't familiar with the test, there are tons of podcasts, websites, and books out there on it. Just do an internet search and you will be overwhelmed with options to understand the Enneagram. I have found that one of the hardest and best numbers on the Enneagram to work with are eights. There's a whole realm to understand the

Enneagram, but basically, eights are people who like to be in charge and know how to get things done. Before I understood the depths of an eight, they used to intimidate the living daylight out of me. I was so hesitant to ever work closely with someone who was an eight because I don't want to be bossed around.

I'm not a bossy person, except when the dishes need to get done or someone left their shoes out for the three millionth time. And I never walk into a room full of people and think I need to be the person in charge.

But I have friends who do. And learning to work with them and understand them has helped me so much when it comes to my perception of God. Why? Because sometimes our human experiences lead us to an unhealthy perception of God.

Some of us have trust issues with God because we like to be in charge. And some of us have trust issues with God because it's just generally hard for us to trust.

* **Which statement best describes you?**

    A. I struggle to trust God because I like to be in charge.

    B. I struggle to trust God because I have trust issues.

As we've studied Noah the last few weeks, it could seem like God was kinda bossy, in charge and not really giving any options. This is true to a certain extent. But the main thing to remember whenever we are studying an Old Testament passage is that everything changed for humanity after Jesus came.

The decision to trust in what God did for humanity on the cross is one to hold on to tightly when doubt starts to make us feel unsettled. One reason I kept these five decisions in this message of *Flooded* so simple was because I wanted you to be able to call them out quickly when you need them the most. You don't have to do this on your own, but you do have to keep making the decisions.

* What will it mean for you in the coming days to decide to remember Who is in charge?

What three things (or more) are you grateful not to be in charge of?

    1. _____

    2. _____

    3. _____

* What is something you wish you were in charge of?

To help ground your trust, look up these verses and fill in the blanks.

    Psalm 46:10: We can trust God because _____.

    Hebrews 13:8: We can trust God because _____.

    Isaiah 26:3: We can trust God because _____.

    Proverbs 3:5–6: We can trust God because _____.

What is something new you learned this week?

Your takeaway for the week?

Seasons of life
come and go,
but God's
faithfulness
remains.

Decision Five:
To Find the Familiar Faithfulness of God

The Certainty of Faith

Read: Chapter 13 of *Flooded* and Genesis 8:20–22.

Write down one thing you are trusting God for today:

Verse-of-the-Week Daily Challenge: In a journal, write out this verse and process what it means to you personally to know that God keeps His promises from generation to generation. How have you seen this in your life?

> Let us hold fast the confession of our hope without wavering, for he who promised is faithful.
>
> Hebrews 10:23

*T*ry to do things that feel normal.

It's been the piece of advice I feel like I've heard in every hard season I've walked through. And I understand. There's something familiar about getting up and getting dressed each day. Taking the kids to school. Going to the grocery store. Sending emails. Checking social media. Making dinner. Doing laundry.

When it feels like life is hard and falling apart, we crave anything and everything that feels . . . familiar. Which is why people suggest routines in a crisis or after a loss. And I'm all for a routine with God: reading, praying, worshiping, etc. But there are times when a routine doesn't cut it.

We become desperate for God to remind us who He is. What He's doing. And how we can experience Him when it feels like doubt has swallowed us whole.

Throughout this study guide, we have defined multiple times where the opposite of faith is doubt. We've decided to make decisions to help us stay on the road of faith. And we've called out our struggles against doubt.

But as we enter this last week of study, I have a slightly opposing thought.

What if the opposite of faith is certainty? Doesn't that sound good?

When I'm hurting and desperate for a touch from God, I really don't want to sort through any more emotions or feelings. I just want to know what I can count on. And here's the good news: With God, there is a lot of certainty.

We've looked a lot at what to do during the storm. But what about when the storm is over and there's a whole life before us that needs to be sorted through? We need certainty.

It's going to be vital to take the time to work through this last decision Noah teaches us:

Decision Five: To find the familiar faithfulness of God

Read Genesis 8:20–22. What did Noah do first when he got off the ark?

Noah has been through a crisis physically and emotionally. The life he had lived for somewhere around six hundred years was no more. When we walk through a crisis and get to the other side, I'm not sure worship and sacrifice are among the first things we would choose to do.

We tend to sit in our grief. We let things settle. But when Noah left the ark, he made a decision to worship and sacrifice.

Notice this isn't something God commanded Noah to do. It was a choice.

Does the passage say if anyone was with Noah? Yes or No

For me, one of the hardest parts about grief and loss is people saying they're here for me, or, my least favorite gesture, "Let me know if you need anything. . . ." While I believe we need people to hold us up, to support and pray for us, there is a tender place in our souls where we will have to figure this out ourselves. It becomes a decision—one we can only make for ourselves: to find God's familiar faithfulness after the storm.

I think it's actually easier to see God's familiar faithfulness IN the storm than in the aftermath, where so much has to be cleaned up and the pain of our new reality becomes ours to bear. I think about the day my brother died. After they took his body away, there was so much to sort through because he had been homeless and I didn't have much information about him at that point. It was like piecing together a puzzle of pain.

* **Think of the last time you experienced a loss of any kind. What were some things that "had" to be done after the loss?**

I'll be honest. I'm feeling a little convicted today as I read about Noah building the altar and making offerings to God. I'm not sure turning to God would have been my first reaction. But this act felt familiar to Noah. He knew God had not left him during this season. And to see Noah's actions aligned with that belief is challenging and convicting. Because it makes me realize that my soul still has a lot of growth to do with God. And that truth is good and holy to recognize and receive.

105

What does Hebrews 13:15 describe as our sacrifice to God?

A. Money

B. Time

C. Love

D. Praise

What is God's promise to Noah in Genesis 8:21?

One verse later (Genesis 8:22) is the first time in the Scriptures we see any reference to seasons. The flood did more than wipe out humanity. It created a whole new seasonal and temperature variations. Many scientists believe this is why, shortly after this, the earth went into the Ice-Age.

Let's go back to our opposing question. *What if the opposite of faith is certainty?* God's faithfulness is something we can be certain about. If Noah is showing us we can experience it from worship and sacrifice, specifically *after* the storm, it's something to pay attention to in our lives.

* **Write down everything you believe about God's faithfulness that is certain:**

In Chapter 13 of *Flooded*, we talked about the promises of God that we can count on. What were the three that I unpacked?

1. _____

2. _____

3. _____

* What are some other promises in Scripture you can count on?

Write down any takeaways you had from chapter 13 of *Flooded*:

Finding Faithfulness

Read: Chapter 14 of *Flooded* and Genesis 9:1–17.

Write down one thing you are trusting God for today:

Verse-of-the-Week Daily Challenge: Write the verse five times in your journal or elsewhere.

> Let us hold fast the confession of our hope without wavering, for he who promised is faithful.
>
> Hebrews 10:23

Typically, on day two of our study, we focus on the verse of the week. We will do that today, but there's a lot more Scripture to cover from Noah's account. So today, you get to do both!

The book of Hebrews was written to be a source of encouragement for the Jews who experienced persecution for their belief in God. Their faith had been flipped upside down, and nothing felt normal to them either.

They were craving God's familiar faithfulness, and the writer of this verse was trying to remind them of this sacred place that never leaves us.

This is one of the many reasons I love the Word of God, because for every hard thing we will walk through on this earth, there's someone who walked through it before us. As we study the Bible, we see its wisdom, encouragement, and truth that applies to us today.

This is why we can declare Hebrews 10:23 for our lives right now: *"Let us hold fast the confession of our hope without wavering, for he who promised is faithful."* Tucked in this verse is the promise of God's familiar faithfulness—both then and today.

Seasons may come and go, but His familiar faithfulness remains. Life will twist and turn, but we can always see His familiar faithfulness if we decide to look for it. We will question and wonder, but our doubts don't change His familiar faithfulness—they simply try to cover it up.

God cannot lie, He never changes His mind, He never forgets His Word, and He has never failed anyone with the fulfillment of His promises. Jesus' death and resurrection never stop existing. It's up to us to look for the familiar faithfulness of God in seasons that feel uncomfortable, unfamiliar, and ever-changing.

Today, our news feeds will be filled with heartache, hard situations, and heavy struggles. It might make us question God's faithfulness, but we can find it through the pages of Noah's account.

What was God's last command to Noah and his family in Genesis 9:1?

Turn to Genesis 1:28 and write out God's command to Adam and Eve.

This command to be fruitful and multiply appears in several other places in the Bible. But I want to make sure we unpack something here. In this context, where God is giving this command to Noah and his family, it is to refill the earth. But not everyone's life plan includes marriage or children. I have several friends who are single, and I see God using them in ways that we would define as being fruitful and multiplying.

* **What are other ways we can "be fruitful and multiply" outside of marriage and having children?**

Turn to Genesis 9:13–17 and summarize the verses:

What was the sign of the covenant?

    A. Water

    B. A rainbow

    C. Rain

    D. Dust

What does verse 16 say God does every time He sees a rainbow?

* **When was the last time you saw a rainbow? Describe it and how it made you feel:**

There is a fresh wind of grace flowing into our lives today through the Holy Spirit. It's not stale, old, or even normal. But it is familiar. And as we worship, praise, and declare His faithfulness over our lives, that wind will feel stronger and stronger. Rainbows are beautiful reminders of God's faithfulness, but we can't just wait for rainbows to show up every day.

Every day we should be expectant and hopeful to experience something new with God. Because we are the ones changing, shifting, growing, maturing, and becoming more like Him each day. Every day, there is a promise from God we can hold on to. Here are a few I would love for you to work through.

1. God is always good.

He doesn't measure up to a standard of goodness. He *is* the standard. Goodness means being like Him, and its definition is derived from His character.

> Oh give thanks to the LORD, for he is good; for his steadfast love endures forever!
>
> 1 Chronicles 16:34

* **What does it mean to you that God is good despite what your circumstances say?**

2. God is everywhere at all times.

The eyes of the LORD are in every place, keeping watch on the evil and the good.

> Proverbs 15:3

* **How does this connect with you, knowing that no matter where you go, God is with you?**

3. God will always be your source of strength.

But they who wait for the LORD shall renew their strength; they shall mount up with wings like eagles; they shall run and not be weary; they shall walk and not faint.

Isaiah 40:31

Hope and faith in the Bible are similar in that they both involve confidence in something unseen. Hope is oriented toward the future, whereas faith can be oriented toward either the present or the future, trusting for something that is currently unseen.

* **What ways do you reach out to God to find strength?**

Write down any takeaways you had from chapter 14 of *Flooded*:

Frustrated but Faithful

Read: Chapter 15 of *Flooded* and Genesis 9:18–29.

Write down one thing you are trusting God for today:

Verse-of-the-Week Daily Challenge: Fill in the blanks today.

Let us _____ fast the _____ of our _____ without _____, for

he who _____ is _____ .

Hebrews 10:23

I was recently thinking about a situation in my life where every bit
of ugly humanity came out of me. A few years ago, in an effort
to make things run a little smoother around our house, I made
my girls ride the bus to school. They were less than pleased because it
was very uncool to ride the bus. Not only that, they had to walk about
a half mile to the bus stop. I know, *What kind of mom am I?!*

One rainy morning I had mercy on their school bus–riding souls and
drove them down to the bus stop on my way to work. The bus pulled
up, pressed on the brakes, and extended its flashing red stop sign. At the

same time, a man whom I learned was running late for work and clearly not paying a bit of attention, continued driving at the same 55-mile-per-hour speed down the road at the exact time my girls were crossing the road to get on the bus. He swerved inches from my daughter and ended up in the cornfield next to us, and then proceeded to turn his car quickly and zoom down our residential dead-end road. He must have thought there was a back way out, but I knew he was trapped.

I couldn't believe my eyes. My whole body was shaking. I got the girls onto the bus, and multiple drivers in nearby cars shouted to me to get his license plate and call the police.

I stood in the middle of the road, hands on my hips, waiting for him to return from his dead-end road trip. He slowly pulled up and rolled his window down and began to apologize in panic. But I wasn't hearing ONE WORD of his reckless apology.

I assure you, by the time I was done lecturing that man, he did not leave my presence thinking I loved Jesus. It was a very human side of Nicki Koziarz. Maybe the most human I've ever been.

I'm sure you can think of a time or two or three when it's been hard to be anything but completely human in a moment of tension, stress, sadness, or disappointment.

I'm so thankful Noah's account ends on such a very human note. Because, let's be real. His faith has looked pretty flawless until this point, according the texts we have studied. Still, it doesn't mean there weren't things happening behind the scenes of Scripture that were very humanly flawed and full of doubt.

Noah's made a little bit of a reckless decision. As we discuss in chapter 14 in *Flooded*, it's not clear how or why he ended up in this place, but regardless, he does. And his very human side comes out.

Read Genesis 9:18–29.

What were some of the possible reasons I shared in chapter 14 for Noah getting drunk?

In verse 23, which two sons covered Noah up?

A. Shem and Ham
B. Japheth and Ham
C. Japheth and Shem

I think it's interesting and important to note the different reactions of each of Noah's sons. Being a mom to three daughters has made me value and appreciate my daughters in different ways. And for sure, no matter what the circumstance, they each have a different reaction toward things. The reflection of verse 23 shows us that Noah had a different relationship with each son. We don't know if there was a long-lasting tension between Noah and Ham, but something was not right, because in the next few verses we see Noah do something that is kind of surprising.

Whom does Noah curse in verse 25? _____

In chapter 14 of *Flooded*, I talk about Noah cursing a relative. What was his relation?

What was one reason Noah spoke the curse I mentioned in chapter 14?

Whom does Noah bless in verses 26 and 27?

In the same passage we see both faith and humanity. Blessings and curses. Good relationships and rocky relationships. All things that could have led Noah down a road of frustration.

I don't know if *frustrated* is the word I'd use to describe how I felt that morning at the bus stop. More like furious. Maybe that's how Noah felt toward Ham. And we won't always get this right. Remember that. If we set ourselves up for a process of perfection, we will only find ourselves in a place of frustration. It's okay to be human.

But it's equally important to understand our human side so we know when we need to call down God's familiar faithfulness and put a stop to the cycles that are leading us in destructive decisions. Noah was a good man who needed some grace in this moment. What all happened? We won't know on this side of eternity. But despite it all, Noah still expressed the faithfulness of God over his family through blessing.

The afternoon after the bus-stop saga, I remembered to pause and thank God for His familiar faithfulness over that day despite all my very human reactions.

In every situation in our lives, there is an opportunity to speak blessings or curses. In every situation we can find the familiar faithfulness of God. But it's up to us to decide to experience it.

Fill in the blanks for Psalm 19:14, and use this as a prayer to end today's study.

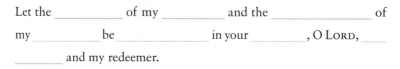

Let the _____ of my _____ and the _____ of
my _____ be _____ in your _____, O Lord, _____
_____ and my redeemer.

Psalm 19:14

Write down any takeaways you had from chapter 15 of *Flooded*:

It's Going to Be Fine

Read: Catch up on anything you missed this week!

Write down one thing you are trusting God for today:

Verse-of-the-Week Daily Challenge: Put this verse somewhere in your home or office. It could be as simple as written on a sticky note, or you can order a beautiful print off the web. But find a way to keep this verse close.

> Let us hold fast the confession of our hope without wavering, for he who promised is faithful.
>
> Hebrews 10:23

This assignment I have been given to teach the Bible requires a lot of flying. But this is a problem because: I DON'T LIKE TO FLY.

I've read every article there is about why planes crash. (Mostly? Human error. Ahhh.) I've also Googled strange sounds, including beeps over the intercom I've heard on planes. A few months ago, I had to board a tiny plane because I was headed to the middle of nowhere. Such places often require small planes, which are typically really bumpy and cause my heart to race. But relief came because I noticed to my left there was a pilot sitting across from me.

I always feel better when there's a pilot in the main cabin because, like seriously, if the plane does crash, he's probably going to be only one who knows how to open one of those emergency exits. Even though we all agree to save EVERYONE'S life if we sit in the exit row. *Liars.* We're all liars just living for a little more leg room in the exit row.

We went through all the typical safety procedures, and then it was time for takeoff.

Normally I have headphones in my ears during takeoff and landing because it helps with the anxiety. But I had forgotten mine. So it was just me, my thoughts, and all the strange noises of the airplane.

As the flight took off, it was pretty smooth. So I took a deep breath and tried to close my eyes. Suddenly, the plane started ROCKING. I'd never experienced anything like it before. Not only was it rocking from side to side, it was rocking up and down, as if something had made the plane lose control. I started to think about all those articles I had read, and I knew, this was it. *Humannnnn errrrrrrror.*

Everyone was a little frightened, but one woman was screaming: "I DON'T WANT TO DIE!!!!!"

Me neither, woman.

My heart was beating fast until I remembered there was a pilot in the row across from me. I glanced over and he was SMILING. *What on earth?* Like, not even fazed by this chaos. He looked at my frightened face and said, "We're fine."

I didn't believe him. And that woman kept screaming.

Finally, the man in charge, Captain Quiet, came on the loudspeaker and said, "So sorry, folks, I could hear we upset a few people with that unexpected turbulence. We're all good, and it looks like it should be a smooth flight from here on out."

After my heart stopped beating three thousand beats per minute, I closed my eyes again.

"We're fine."

Sometimes we just need someone to look at us in the midst of chaos and say those words: *It's fine.*

Honestly, this is what God's familiar faithfulness does. It reminds us that it's fine. But it's hard to hear this, right? Because it feels like the world is spinning in the wrong direction. It feels bumpy and hard, and there are all kinds of shouts of doubt around us.

We're almost done with this study. But you've been in training your whole life for this moment. God's been showing you His familiar faithfulness all along the way, and today we're going to take some time to look back but also make a plan for looking ahead.

* **On the timeline below, list as many situations as you can remember from the time you were a child until today, where you recognize God's familiar faithfulness.**

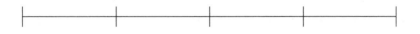

* **Now, list five things you want to accomplish in your lifetime.**

1. _____

2. _____

3. _____

4. _____

5. _____

* **How do you see your past shaping your future?**

How will doubt convince you those things are not possible?

How could God's familiar faithfulness carry you from one challenging situation to the next?

In chapter 15 of *Flooded*, I shared about Kennedy's journey to ride a horse again. Some of you may feel like for the first time in a long time you are ready to get back up and dream some dreams. Or do some things that look impossible to the world but just right in God's eyes. What you will do from this day forward matters. There is a resistance fighting for your soul to not remember God's faithfulness in your life.

If I could only tell you six things about this today, here they are:

1. Write down one thing every day in which you experienced God's faithfulness.
2. Never stop telling people about the things God has done for you. Your faith will inspire theirs.
3. Take a big step. Do something different, unknown. Of course, pray about it first, but when you feel a nudging you just can't get rid of, go.
4. Continue to read about God's faithfulness through the Scriptures. Read about it again and again.
5. Whenever you experience God's faithfulness, pause and thank Him. Recognize Him in your life and watch Him keep showing up in ways you can't explain.
6. Remember, it doesn't have to make sense for it to work. Nothing about the account of Noah made a whole lot of sense. Yet God's familiar faithfulness led him.

Next week we're going to put these decisions to work for you to build a life based on faith, not fear. We're going to take this a little further than Noah's account and see what happened to him, his family, and his legacy. But for today, just know that I think you have done incredible soul work here. All of this has felt really hard for me personally to sort through, and I'm sure for you, as well. But you did it. And I'm here for it. And for you.

We've made it through all five decisions. Can you write each of them out without looking back? Try below!

1. _____

2. _____

3. _____

4. _____

5. _____

* **What is your takeaway for this week of study?**

* **What is one new thing you learned?**

God has a
legacy for you,
and He will
show you
step by step.

The Legacy You'll Leave

SESSION 6 VIDEO STUDY NOTES

What Are You Building?

Read: Genesis 10.

Write down one thing you are trusting God for today:

No new Verse-of-the-Week Daily Challenge this week! But I encourage you to go back and review the verses we studied with each decision.

It's kinda crazy to think that it's only nine chapters into the entire Bible when everything changes. By Genesis 10, a whole new world emerges. It's also kinda crazy to think that literally every chapter in the Bible after Genesis 9 is the result of one man's obedience. Humanity would have been wiped out if Noah had chosen not to listen to God.

Here's a hard question . . . have you ever thought about what people would say about you after you die? I don't want to get all morbid and doom and gloom on our last week of this study guide, but the reality is, we are all one day closer to reaching our final breath here on earth. And whether we realize it or not, we're all building something with our lives.

Noah built his life on faith.

But what we're about to see in this next part of our study is that his family didn't necessarily follow his footsteps after he died.

I'm sure today's reading of Genesis 10 might feel a little . . . yawn, yawn. Especially compared to the excitement of the last few chapters we studied. But genealogies are important, and they actually teach us a lot. Let's dig into this just a little.

What were Noah's sons' names?

A. Shem, Ham, and Japheth

B. Ham, Shem, and Japheth

C. Japheth, Shem, and Ham

(Smiles. Hopefully you circled A, B, and C.)

According to Genesis 10:2, what were the names of Japheth's sons?

1. _____

2. _____

3. _____

4. _____

5. _____

6 _____

7. _____

Genesis 10:6 lists Ham's sons. What were their names?

1. _____

2. _____

3. _____

4. _____

Last but not least, Genesis 10:22 lists Shem's sons. What were their names?

1. _____

2. _____

3. _____

4. _____

5. _____

I won't make you list out all the grandsons' names because, mercy, it's getting to be a lot of people to track. But there's one name, in particular, we should know. That is Ham's son, Cush. Cush had a son named Nimrod. And we need to take a few minutes to understand who he is, because it will tie in to tomorrow's study.

According to the *Word Biblical Commentary*, Nimrod's name can be translated as "we shall rebel,"[1] possibly foreshadowing Genesis 11:1–9, which we'll get to tomorrow.

Nimrod is just three generations from Noah. His great-grandson. But before we dig any further into this, stop and think about your generational lines.

For some of you, you can very easily identify the people who were two or even three generations before you in your family line. Others may not have that knowledge, so looking back might feel challenging. But all of us can look ahead.

Whether you have children or not, God is building something in you that has the potential to reach into two generations ahead of you. Because faith is just that amazing. It can do more than we could ever ask, dream, or imagine (Ephesians 3:20).

---

1. Gordon Wenham, *Word Biblical Commentary, Vol. 1: Genesis 1–15* (Nashville: Thomas Nelson, 1987), 243.

Many people define a *legacy* as something of high monetary value being passed from one generation to the next—an inheritance. But it is so much more. Let's spend some time today on this to help you define your own legacy.

* **What three words would you want people to use to describe your life?**

    1. ....

    2. ....

    3. ....

What things in your life keep you from being the person described above?

Read Psalm 145:4. When you look at your life today, what are you doing or investing in to fulfill Psalm 145:4 through your life?

* **What are you spending time on that doesn't contribute to building your legacy?**

Here's the thing. You may not even know what the Lord is doing through your life right now. But we can trust that there is something. None of us is here to do nothing. God has a purpose for you, and He will show it to you step by step.

It's so important to me as you wrap up this study that you not only understand how Noah made these decisions but that you follow after the legacy of faith he left for us. Each day this week I'm asking you some questions based on these five decisions. Hopefully this daily activity will help make these decisions stick and become part of your daily routine.

Decision One: To walk with God
How are you walking with God today?

Decision Two: To listen to God
What is God saying to you today?

Decision Three: To rise above the doubt
What is doubt trying to say to you?

Decision Four: To remember Who is in charge
How did you experience God's plan and commands yesterday?

Decision Five: To find the familiar faithfulness of God
What is one thing from yesterday you remember as God's faithfulness?

Whom Are You Building For?

Read: Genesis 11:1–4.

Write down one thing you are trusting God for today:

Sometimes we find ourselves in situations where it feels impossible to have wisdom, direction, and discernment about what to do next.

Which is exactly how I felt one morning.

There wasn't anything tragically wrong. I hadn't gone through a major life change. I just didn't know what step to take next as I looked at my to-do list of prayed-through possibilities.

I sat at my simple white desk in my office with the bright white walls and big windows. The simplicity and light of this room normally fills me with peace as I work. But sudden anxiety made this bright space seem as if a dark cloud quickly moved to cover the brightness.

It brought to mind *all* the questions:

What if I get the next step wrong?

What if I miss what God has for me?

What if I am not brave enough to do what I need to do next?

It's often these questions we ask ourselves that lead to the greatest thoughts of doubt, discouragement, and defeat.

But there's a saying: "Show me your friends, and I'll show you your future." It reminds me of today's key verse: "Get all the advice and instruction you can, so you will be wise the rest of your life" (Proverbs 19:20 NLT). As we surround ourselves with people who reflect God, their wisdom can help guide us toward our next step.

So I texted the wisest friend I know and asked if I could get her perspective about the things on my list. Instead of texting back what she thought I should do, she asked me three important questions.

Questions that helped me change the way I was looking at the list.

Questions I want to share with you if you're also in a season of seeking.

Questions that offer the chance to reflect godly wisdom and that I hope will encourage you too.

Question One: *Who are the people you are here for?*

This is important because we can start to think we're here for everyone, all the time. But the reality is, God has placed a burden inside of you for a specific set of people here on this earth. Figure out who they are, and then move on to question two.

* **Who are the people you are here for?**

Question Two: *What are you supposed to give them?*

Each of us has a unique gift to bring to this world. The people you're here for need what you have to give. Whether it be time, encouragement, prayer, teaching, or a dozen other possibilities, never think this world has everything it needs. It needs what you have to give.

* **What are you supposed to give them?**

Question Three: *What gives you the most energy when you put energy into it?*

There are certain things we have to do in life that don't necessarily feel life-giving, and yet we have to do them anyway. But your God-assignments should make you feel like you're alive and ready to do it again and again and again.

* **What gives you the most energy when you put energy into it?**

Let these three questions turn into prayers. And slowly, God will reveal where to direct your focus on your own list of possibilities. When God gives you a vision to build a legacy, there are people involved. It's not just for our name's sake.

Noah's descendants decided to build something for themselves, not others. A legacy was being built, but we're about to see how it didn't work out too well for one particular person.

What does Genesis 11:4 say the people wanted to do?

What does Genesis 11:3 say they were going to make it out of?

A. Wood
B. Stone
C. Bricks

There are many interesting perspectives as to why this group of people would decide to do this. A lot of it has to do with pride, thinking they could actually build something to reach heaven. But some of it could have been fear. After all, the account of the flood had been passed down at least two generations. Perhaps they feared another flood would come, and this would be the only way they could be saved.

Whatever their reasoning, we know that this was a strong statement against God.

What did God command them to do in Genesis 9:1?

How was the building of the Tower of Babel disobedient to that command?

* **How could not taking the time to understand the people God has called you to reach impact your legacy?**

There's so much more to unpack with this, and we will . . . tomorrow. But remember, each day during this last week of our study guide, we're taking the time to sort through the five decisions.

Take a few minutes today and answer the questions below on your daily decision challenge.

Decision One: To walk with God
What is God teaching you as you walk with Him?

Decision Two: To listen to God
What is something you can clearly identify as an instruction from the Lord?

Decision Three: To rise above the doubt
How is doubt trying to detour you today?

Decision Four: To remember Who is in charge
Are you struggling to trust God today? If yes, explain why below.

Decision Five: To find the familiar faithfulness of God
What is something you can see in someone else's life as a reflection of God's faithfulness?

DAY 3

How Will You Fight
for Your Legacy?

Read: Genesis 11:5–9.

Write down one thing you are trusting God for today:

We are at an end, of sorts, of the account of Noah. The reality is, his legacy goes way past where we will close the Scriptures today. But what you will see today is that humanity was a mess at the beginning of this study, and it's still a mess. And where we find ourselves in the midst of God's story of humanity reveals . . . humans are still a mess. In the south, we'd say a *hot mess*.

And until Jesus returns, we will stay a mess. But you and I can at least be a *faithful* mess.

* **Why do you think God is so frustrated with humanity again in verse 6?**

Write out Genesis 11:7:

One thing to point out about this verse is that "let us" is most likely a reference to the Trinity. More evidence the Trinity has always existed.

What does verse 7 say God would do to their language?

A. Made it clear
B. Confused it
C. Made them silent

Summarize what happened in verses 7, 8, and 9:

* **If Noah had been alive to see all this unfold, what do you think his thoughts could have been?**

If you had access to my thoughts for a day, I think you'd be surprised how many negative thoughts pass through my brain.
Things like:
Not good enough.
Not smart enough.
Not worthy enough.
Just not enough.

I've never been a highly confident person. But I also wouldn't say I have extremely low self-confidence. I find myself somewhere in between, bouncing between the high and low. I know what the Bible says about who I am, and I know who God thinks I am. But I still find myself teetering between what I *know* versus what I *feel*.

And if I'm honest, sometimes what I'm feeling comes out in a way that doubt shines through. How we fight for our legacy comes down to one command given by God:

> "The second is this: 'Love your neighbor as yourself.' There is no commandment greater than these."
>
> Mark 12:31 NIV

After years of wrestling with self-doubt, I've come to understand it's a *love* issue.

One reason why I think we struggle so much to live out the second greatest commandment is because, honestly, we struggle to love ourselves the right way.

There's a saying: *Hurt people hurt people.*

We could insert a dozen other words into this phrase, such as people who struggle to love themselves, struggle to live out their legacy.

Somehow, the message to love yourself like God does was turned into pride. People with too much confidence in themselves were deemed arrogant or full of themselves. Nobody wanted that.

So we ran the opposite direction, creating this unhealthy consequence in thinking low of others. But that route seems to have left us in disobedience to this command. If Jesus said loving our neighbor was the *second* greatest commandment, we need to understand what the first is. It's found in Mark 12:30:

> "Love the Lord your God with all your heart and with all your soul and with all your mind and with all your strength" (NIV).

Thankfully, God doesn't just expect us to "get this." He provides so much Scripture for us to fill our minds with His love, in order to live out His commands. But Noah had commands that led to his legacy, and so do we. This verse is one of them. Let's take some time to unpack it.

1. Love God with all your _heart_.

What we receive is what we can give. Daily, we need to receive this unending love God has for us. Receiving what we need is the only way we don't run "dry" in our ability to give love to others.

* **What does it look like for you to love God with all your heart?**

2. Love God with all your _soul_.

Our souls are a complicated place. One way we can love God with our souls is to seek repentance, a daily cleansing. The more we receive God's forgiveness, the more we can offer forgiveness to others.

* **What does it look like for you to love God with all your soul?**

3. Love God with all your _mind_.

As we think of ourselves how God thinks of us, it becomes easier to think of others like God thinks of them. God is not the author of anyone unworthy or unlovable. May we take captive these thoughts and replace them with the thoughts God has for us.

* **What does it look like for you to love God with all your mind?**

4. Love God with all your _strength_.

Each day we get up and keep going. Strength isn't a place of perfection but a place of perseverance. When we don't give up on God, it allows us to have an extra dose of grace to not give up on ourselves or on others.

✴ **What does it look like to love God with all your strength?**

If it feels hard today to fight for our legacies, maybe we start by loving God and ourselves. Let's receive what we need—so we can give to others what they need. Then we can live out Mark 12:31 and watch the world around us change, one step of love at a time.

Below is the daily decision challenge we are doing this week. Take the time to wrestle with these decisions and questions. Repetition is the best way to make something stick!

Decision One: To walk with God
How are you walking with God today?

Decision Two: To listen to God
What is God saying to you today?

Decision Three: To rise above the doubt
What is doubt trying to say to you?

Decision Four: To remember Who is in charge
How did you experience God's plan and commands yesterday?

Decision Five: To find the familiar faithfulness of God
What is one thing from yesterday you remember as God's faithfulness?

You Finished Well

Read: (You are DONE.)

Write down one thing you are trusting God for today:

We did it! You have studied all I know how to teach you about Noah, his life, and his legacy. You have done the hard work, and I'm so incredibly proud of you. But I know the real work begins from this day on. It's one thing to tackle a struggle together, but it's another thing to step forward on your own and keep going.

My hopes for this final day of our study guide is that this would be a page you will revisit from time to time. It's a refresher page of sorts. A place to turn to when you need to be reminded of all God revealed to you during this study.

I think at the end of our lives we all want those words said about us . . . "You finished well." And I know you will. Life has thrown you curve balls, hard stuff, and things that feel very unfair. I wish I could tell you there will be no more hard things after this. But there will be. For you and for me.

The difference is, we are equipped with so much truth to help us rise above the doubt every time the waters of life get rocky. You know, this process of learning to stop sinking in my own doubt stemmed from the greatest place of grief I've experienced. Noah taught me that there is life to be lived on the other side of deep grief.

As I've wrapped up writing this study guide, I'm approaching the one-year mark of my brother's suicide. It's been painful to look back over this last year and remember all that I walked through. But I am here. And my soul is better because of the places I've let my grief lead us through this book and study guide. Where there is much pain, there is much power. And you and I are not the sum of our pain. We are the evidence of Jesus' power on the cross.

This hard work we've done through the book and the study guide has turned into holy work.

So I will keep rising. And you will too. And one day, together, we'll reach eternity, where we will meet our Jesus face-to-face and all will finally be made right.

One of the prayers I pray frequently after teaching the Bible at an event is, "God, please seal this Word in our hearts." I pray this over you right now. Use the section below as a time of prayer and reflection.

Decision One: To walk with God
Where did we see this lived out with Noah?

What stood out to you the most about this decision?

Write out the verse you studied connected to this decision:

Decision Two: To listen to God
Where did we see this lived out with Noah?

Describe what it will mean for you to continue to listen to God.

Write out the verse you studied connected to this decision:

Decision Three: To rise above the doubt
Where did we see this lived out with Noah?

Create a plan of action—what you'll do the next time doubt slips in.

Write out the verse you studied connected to this decision:

Decision Four: To remember Who is in charge
Where did we see this lived out with Noah?

What is that one thing you are still trusting God will do in your life?

Write out the verse you studied connected to this decision:

Decision Five: To find the familiar faithfulness of God
Where did we see this lived out with Noah?

Write out the verse you studied connected to this decision:

Who are the people you will keep in your circle of influence that will help you find God's familiar faithfulness?

Nicki Koziarz is a two-time ECPA bestselling author and speaker with Proverbs 31 Ministries. She speaks nationally at conferences, retreats, and meetings, and hosts her own podcast. An evangelist at heart, Nicki inspires others to become the best version of who God created them to be. Nicki and her husband and three daughters own a small farm just outside of Charlotte, North Carolina, they affectionately call the Fixer Upper Farm.

More from Nicki Koziarz

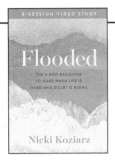

Deepen your ability to rise above doubt with this powerful video series that builds on *Flooded* and the *Flooded Study Guide*. From her Fixer Upper Farm, Nicki Koziarz walks you through the hard and holy work that leads to trusting God more and more.

Flooded Video Study

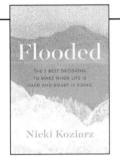

"A powerful, life-changing read for anyone who has ever struggled to believe when life is hard."
—Susan Davidson, *Flooded* focus group participant

Flooded

BETHANYHOUSE

 Stay up to date on your favorite books and authors with our free e-newsletters. Sign up today at bethanyhouse.com.

 facebook.com/BHPnonfiction

 @bethany_house

 @bethany_house_nonfiction

Proverbs 31
MINISTRIES

Know the Truth. Live the Truth.
It changes everything.

If you were inspired by *Flooded* and the *Flooded Study Guide* and desire to deepen your own personal relationship with Jesus Christ, Proverbs 31 Ministries has just what you are looking for.

Proverbs 31 Ministries exists to be a trusted friend who will take you by the hand and walk by your side, leading you one step closer to the heart of God through:

- Free online daily devotions
- First 5 Bible study app
- Online Bible Studies
- Podcast

- COMPEL Writer Training
- She Speaks Conference
- Books and resources

Our desire is to help you to know the Truth and live the Truth. Because when you do, it changes everything.

For more information about Proverbs 31 Ministries,
visit: www.Proverbs31.org.